Christmas USA

Mary D. Lankford

Illustrated by Karen Dugan

Collins

An Imprint of HarperCollinsPublishers

With fond memories I give my heartfelt thanks to Meredith Charpentier for her creative guidance on this project from its inception and for many additional months. Thanks to Leslie Tryon and J. Fowler for showing us the history and beauty of the Monterey, California, area. Special thanks to John C. Briley for creating gingerbread houses, growing peanuts, creating the crafts, and cooking the recipes.

With love for Barbara and Robert Bertoldo for their sincerity,
encouragement, and friendship

—M.D.L.

For Eliza Jane and Hope Marguerite Desmarais,
and their parents, John and Cheryl Desmarais,
who carry the Christmas spirit with them year-round,
and with love always

—K.D.

Collins is an imprint of HarperCollins Publishers.

Christmas USA
Text copyright © 2006 by Mary D. Lankford
Illustrations copyright © 2006 by Karen Dugan

Manufactured in China.

Library of Congress Cataloging-in-Publication Data

Lankford, Mary D. Christmas USA / Mary D. Lankford ; illustrated by Karen Dugan. — 1st ed.
ISBN-10: 0-688-15012-8 — ISBN-10: 0-06-000861-X (lib. bdg.)
ISBN-13: 978-0-688-15012-9 — ISBN-13: 978-0-06-000861-1 (lib. bdg.)
1. Christmas—United States—History—Juvenile literature. 2. United States—Social life and customs—
Juvenile literature. I. Title.
GT4986.A1L37 2006
394.2663—dc22
                                                                                                    2005013234

Typography by Elynn Cohen   1 2 3 4 5 6 7 8 9 10   ❖   First Edition

Contents

 # Introduction

You may think that celebrations of Christmas are the same across the United States. As I journeyed across our country researching customs, I found that, while there *are* many similarities, cultural traditions rich with meaning remain. This book contains just a few of the celebrations and traditions I discovered.

In my youth most families visited grandparents who lived in the same town or on a nearby farm. Times change, and now families may be far away. Recently I flew to Washington on Christmas Eve and was met by three excited grandchildren and my son. We piled presents, a smoked ham, and luggage into the car, keeping the tradition of visiting relatives at Christmas.

My parents used to tell stories of early married days when they found it difficult to spare six dollars to purchase a rocking chair for my grandfather. That amount of money seems small today, but in the Depression years of the 1930s, most families were suffering financial hardships.

The lighting displays of today were unknown in my childhood. Our family always made a special trip to Denton city hall in north Texas to view the blue lights outlining the building. At home my sister and I were fascinated by the candle-shaped tree lights; bubbles inside the lights kept rising to the top. Our brief list of gifts might have included a new game such as Monopoly or pick-up sticks, jacks, or a top. We longed for dolls named after the movie star Shirley Temple or Princess Elizabeth. The most popular doll was a "storybook doll." Santa brought these small dolls in boxes covered with polka dots.

No matter how hard we wished, our Christmas was rarely white with snow in Texas. We enjoyed the season in other ways. There were pecans to crack and shell for Christmas baking. The entire house was filled with the aroma of baking fruitcakes, cookies, and yeast breads. My mother was a very good cook, and my dad was always trying to find the newly baked fruitcake. They pretended to argue about how long the cake must "season" before it could be cut. Tangerines were usually available only at Christmas. The fragrant scent of tangerines is still my most powerful Christmas memory.

Not long ago I witnessed a wonderful celebration near my home, a reenactment of events in a city that most of us know only through the brief description in the Bible. The members of the church created a world where visitors could interact with costumed people and events of Biblical times. For one evening it seemed we were no longer in a church in Plano, Texas, but that we had walked through the gates of ancient Bethlehem. We purchased small gifts in the market. In the stable sheep and cows stood patiently as parents with a small baby played the roles of Mary, Joseph, and the infant Jesus. The comment from my granddaughter Caitlyn was "This is the best thing you have ever taken me to see!"

As all the volunteers who contributed their time and effort to bring us this wonderful experience know, perhaps the best way to celebrate is in the spirit of the apostle Paul, who quoted Jesus: "It is more blessed to give than to receive" (Acts 20:35).

Northeast

From Pennsylvania to Maine, there are many hints of early American history. Signs direct visitors to historic sites found at every turn in the road. You may see a sign pointing to the home of Benjamin Franklin. The next corner may reveal a town hall where events that shaped our government actually took place. It is like stepping back in time. These opportunities to view history up close reinforce pride in our American heritage. Like many other states, those in the Northeast celebrate their history with re-creations of long-ago Christmases.

In the 1600s, during the early colonial years, Christmas was not as joyful a holiday as it is today. In 1659 the Puritans of Massachusetts outlawed any celebration of Christmas. Can you imagine attending school on Christmas Day? Although the law was repealed in 1681, as late as 1828 a teacher wrote in her diary, "Happened to think that this day is Christmas, but seeing none of my scholars take note of it, I thought if I did, I should appear rather odd, & so I let it pass." In time, families celebrated the holiday with dinners and decorations of evergreen boughs. There were no stockings by the fireplace, and no Santa Claus. Just a small piece of holly or fir might make the room more festive.

Christmas became a time for celebration by the mid-nineteenth century. The observance may have been prayers of thankfulness for obtaining basic needs such as food, clothing, and shelter. Gifts were few and very simple. The warmth of a good fire, family close by, and the promise of a better future were the gifts early immigrants cherished.

Native Americans had introduced the Pilgrims to a new food. This was a small, slightly sour, red berry that grew in nearby marshy areas. Can you guess what it was? The cranberry. Cranberries served as a jelly or a relish with chopped oranges and sugar added to a Christmas feast. The red berries were also strung together to decorate early Christmas trees.

Today in Portsmouth, New Hampshire, people re-create a Christmas of the mid-1800s in an annual event, held on the first two weekends in December. Portsmouth began as a settlement called Strawbery Banke. The name and early spelling describe an area that was covered with strawberry plants. Thirty-seven restored buildings remain on their original sites. As in Christmases past, Strawbery Banke is aglow with flickering candles in eleven hundred glass lanterns beside the dirt paths. Visitors can see the homes of rich merchants and government officials, and the simple homes of laborers, who made barrels and other necessities of life, bedecked for Christmas. Young people dressed in costumes of the mid-nineteenth century are eager to explain to visitors what a servant or owner of the house would be doing to celebrate the holiday.

Southeast

Our country is outlined on the southeast by states that have one border formed by either the Gulf Coast or the Atlantic Ocean. Rivers in this region have such magical-sounding names as Alabama, Arkansas, Mississippi, Ocmulgee, Suwannee, and Tennessee. These waterways were the first highways of Indians and pioneers.

Louisiana, explored by the French, was named for their king, Louis XIV. The post of St. Agustín, now called St. Augustine, Florida, was one of many attempts by Spaniards to establish the power of their country on this continent.

European influence is seen in a nighttime Christmas celebration on top of levees holding back the Mississippi River. Pyramids, twenty feet high and twelve feet across, are packed with sugarcane, willow limbs, and cardboard, then burned. This reflects an ancient custom of building fires to encourage the return of longer days during the winter solstice. Legends tell of these lights guiding paddle wheel boats on the foggy river, and showing people the way to midnight mass on Christmas Eve. These sugarcane fires, blazing orange and yellow between Baton Rouge and New Orleans, also light the way for Papa Noel, or Santa Claus.

For the past twenty-five years, thousands of volunteers in the city of Demopolis, Alabama, have hosted a festival called Christmas on the River. Early in the day, a street parade features children in oversized papier-mâché heads costumed as storybook characters, marching bands from neighboring towns, fire engines, and floats that show Santa's workshop and a variety of Nativity scenes.

Later there are a Fair on the Square, a beauty pageant, choir concerts, plays, a barbecue cook-off, a quilt display in the public library, and an opportunity to eat "crock on a stick," which is alligator shish kebob.

At twilight crowds move toward the Tombigbee River. Boats laden with large double-sided wooden shapes slowly become visible in the water. As darkness envelops the river, spectators soon see images of elves, Santa, the Three Wise Men, and other familiar Christmas figures outlined in thousands of brightly colored lights that shimmer in the dark river water.

Months of planning are necessary to the success of these Christmas celebrations. The one factor that cannot be controlled is the weather. A vital cash crop of southern states, the peanut, is also affected by weather.

Those of us who grew up in southern states called peanuts "goober peas." Dr. George Washington Carver developed hundreds of products that could be made from parts of the peanut plant. Peanut butter, introduced in 1904, immediately became a favorite food. As a child, I loved Christmas baking. I'd roll peanut-butter cookie dough into small balls, then, using a fork, slightly flatten and mark the tops with a criss-cross design.

Great Lakes

A map of the east and north-central states clearly shows huge bodies of water called the Great Lakes that dominate the area. In fact, all of these states have a lake as one or more of their borders, except for Minnesota, which has twenty thousand lakes within its boundaries. An easy way to remember the names of the Great Lakes is to imagine homes floating on the water. Think of the acronym HOMES: H for Lake Huron, O for Lake Ontario, M for Lake Michigan, E for Lake Erie, and S for Lake Superior.

Although forestry is no longer a major industry in this region, Michigan, Wisconsin, and Ohio rank third, fifth, and sixth as producers of Christmas trees. Now raised on plantations, Christmas trees have become a big business as thousands of spruces, pines, and firs from the region are sent out across the country.

The tree, a symbol of life, is such a part of Christmas celebrations that the idea of Christmas without a tree seems impossible. However, most homes of the earliest immigrants in America had no tree. German immigrants brought this tradition to the New World. In 1747 the German Moravians created a tree made from a wooden pyramid covered with boughs of evergreens. Christmas trees, used inside the home, were not on a stand, but were hung upside down. Most families that wanted a tree cut one in nearby woods. Selling trees started in the 1800s, in New York, when Mark Carr brought two oxsleds of trees from forests up the Hudson River to New York City.

German immigrants also popularized artificial feather trees. Called "trees with wings," they became popular in the mid-nineteenth century.

They were constructed, in a time-consuming process, by attaching dyed goose and turkey feathers to a frame constructed of wire and wood. In the 1930s a New York company started manufacturing cellophane trees. In the 1950s trees were made of paper, wire, cloth, and visca, a synthetic straw.

A Christmas tree in every home was not commonplace until the 1930s. Today it is estimated that approximately 36 million American families enjoy the beauty of a real Christmas tree.

We are not destroying forests when we enjoy a real tree. Most Christmas trees are grown for one purpose—to be cut and sold. For each tree cut, two or three new trees are planted.

Frequently, cities and communities use a Christmas tree as the central focus for their holiday celebrations. Lansing, Michigan, hosts a Festival of Trees. This event often includes a display of trees, decorated by civic groups or schools, a teddy bear tea, and a display of arts and crafts. For many of us, the fresh, clean fragrance of a pine, spruce, or fir tree is linked with our memories of Christmas.

Mountain States

The name of the northerly mountain state Montana is from the Spanish word *montaña*, or "mountain." The rugged Rocky Mountains stretch across Montana, then south through parts of Idaho, Wyoming, Nevada, Utah, and Colorado. "America the Beautiful" describes mountains as "purple majesties." *Majestic* is the perfect word to describe the sight of these mountains silhouetted against the sky and the vistas that open once you reach the mountaintop.

Mountains are important to our nation and our lives. Weather is influenced when mountains block circulating air masses. Trees are cut from mountain forests to provide wood for building homes. Rich mineral deposits are dug from mountains to be made into tools, cooking utensils, and other necessities.

About forty thousand of the immigrants who forged trails through the mountains of Wyoming, Idaho, Utah, and Colorado were children. Their lives on the mountain frontier were continual struggles. Winter was always a dangerous time. In January 1888 a storm, later called the Schoolchildren's Storm, caught children in school or on their way home. This storm caused the deaths of more than two hundred youngsters.

Christmas, if it was celebrated at all, may have included a little more food for the day.

In 1859 Americans rushed to Colorado seeking gold and to Nevada to mine for silver. Christmas came during the slack winter season for mining and usually lasted from December 25 through January 1. Immigrants in mining camps from the Cornwall area of England continued their tradition of caroling. The *Black Hills Daily Times* newspaper reported:

"Our Christmas has come and gone. . . . There was nothing on the surface to distinguish it from a reign of dullness back in a rural village during harvest time. This condition of things doesn't argue well for a mining metropolis. It is a sure indication of the poverty which has overtaken the 'boys and girls.'"

Christmas for early settlers in isolated mountain regions was frequently celebrated with a tree cut from the forest and bedecked with handmade, simple decorations. Most miners and trappers carried a pot or crock of sourdough starter with them. Some families passed down their starter from generation to generation. The starter was a never-ending source for hotcakes, biscuits, and bread. Because so many meals depended upon sourdough starter, these oldtimers were nicknamed "sourdoughs." Even Christmas bread was probably made from sourdough!

It is estimated that at one time, there were almost ten million elk in North America. These large elk herds were eventually reduced to less than a hundred thousand animals. The conflict between people wanting to use the mountains for recreation and exploration for minerals continues to threaten the large areas needed for elk to forage for food. In Jackson, Wyoming, at the National Elk Refuge, you can take elk sleigh rides, if snow conditions permit.

Plains States

Settlers to the Plains region gained skills in surviving with little water. They adapted to vast open expanses that provided few trees for shelter or firewood. These pioneers discovered the land was rich and fertile. Although great storms may come raging across the land with rain or sudden blizzards, midwestern farmers continue to provide our nation with bountiful crops of wheat, corn, oats, potatoes, and sugar beets and to raise livestock. Food from their efforts may even be part of your own Christmas dinner.

In the 1870s North Dakota, still considered a young state, had about twenty-five hundred residents. Bismarck, its capital, was named for the German chancellor at that time, Otto von Bismarck. For the 1970 census, 15 percent of North Dakota's people listed German as their native tongue.

Just as they had in the Great Lakes region, German immigrants brought the Christmas tree and other traditions to the Plains states.

The style of tree decorations eventually changed from homemade to store bought. The earliest ornaments were simple and were often edible, like cookies or popcorn. By 1870 toy makers of Nuremberg, Germany, were manufacturing tin ornaments shaped like stars, crosses, and flowers. These lightweight ornaments, hung by a thread, would spin slowly from the motion of heated air from candles on the tree. Other ornaments, made of silver- and gold-embossed cardboard, were very detailed, and shaped like dogs, toys, ships, musical instruments, and a favorite German Christmas food, carp.

German people, inventors of silver foil icicles, also made small wool dolls, wire stars, and butterflies. Glass ornaments similar to those used today were first made in Europe by German and Czechoslovakian glass bead makers. The decoration at the top of the Christmas tree might have been an angel, a large tin star, or a hand-blown glass *point*. The points were a series of balls joined together with a reflector within each round shape. In the small German town of Lauscha, each home became a small factory creating glass Christmas tree ornaments. The entire family assisted in the process of blowing the glass, silvering inside the ball, dipping in lacquer for color, and placing metal caps on the *pike*, or stem.

Some immigrants brought treasured Christmas tree ornaments from their homeland. Ornaments were considered a "top cargo" for shipment to the United States. After a ship was filled with as much heavy cargo as possible, the lightweight ornaments were used to take up the top space without adding weight.

Immigrants who came to this region long ago helped create traditions still enjoyed today. Their heritage has given us Christmas trees, beautiful glass ornaments, and holiday treats that remind us of past Christmases.

Southwest

Many people in this area claim a Mexican, Spanish, Native American, or European heritage. Many geographical names reflect Spanish influence, such as El Camino Real, or The Royal Road, the oldest road in the United States.

In 1539 Spanish adventurers, seeking the legendary seven cities of gold, came to this area and found a land already occupied by Native Americans. Indians had domesticated the turkey and were growing corn, beans, and squash for food, as well as cotton for weaving blankets. They were called by many names, among them Wichita, Tankawa, Caddo, and Pueblo.

The Pueblo culture's deep respect for nature is expressed through many art forms, including weaving, pottery, and dancing. At Jemez Pueblo and many other pueblos, Christmas Day is spent dancing. Christmas dances are based on the winter dances performed long before the Spanish conquistadors arrived. In ceremonies that are sacred to the Pueblos, drummers accompany reindeer dancers, costumed with deer head masks, feathers, and spruce boughs. Today Santa Claus may accompany the drummer and give candy canes to spectators!

The Christmas season begins with a *piñon*, or pine, bonfire. At Cochiti Pueblo, beehive-shaped adobe ovens may be found behind many houses. On Christmas Eve the villagers visit the home of the family hosting the small statue of baby Jesus for the season. This small clay figure, normally found in the local church, visits only one family each year. Following midnight mass at the Catholic Church, visitors to this home are fed chicken stew, *posole* (a stew that usually includes corn or hominy and green chiles), chili, and bread cookies.

Just as a star was bright over the stable in Bethlehem, the clear air of the Southwest seems to bring the glow of stars within arm's reach. Light, a symbol and reminder of the Christ Child, is seen throughout the Southwest. The glow of *las luminarias*, or festival lights, are seen in windows, on sidewalks, and outlining the rooftops of adobe homes. Luminarias are symbols of the fires shepherds used for warmth, light, and protection on the night angels appeared with news of the Christ Child.

Since 1987 the entire community of Marshall, Texas, has worked to create a spectacle consisting of more than six million electric lights.

It was Jesus who said, "I am the light of the world. He that followeth me shall not walk in darkness, but shall have the light of life" (John 8:12). The hope his birth brought to the world continues to bring joy throughout our country.

Pacific States

The highest point in the United States is in Alaska. Death Valley, California, is below sea level. The only rainforests in the continental United States are found in Oregon and Washington. Icy glaciers of Alaska contrast with the tropical climate of Hawaii. The only state that ever sees the sun directly overhead is Hawaii. All these states have one thing in common. Each has shores touched by the Pacific Ocean.

In December 1778 Captain Cook arrived at what would become our most westerly state, Hawaii. The captain was given gifts of fruit, hogs, and a goose. We can suppose the first Europeans who were in Hawaiian waters around Christmas feasted on goose.

In 1847 a large Christmas celebration was held at Punahou School. Around the dining table, which stretched the length of two rooms, 101 guests were seated. Future rulers of Hawaii Walania Kamaka'eha (Queen Liliuokalani) and Alexander Liholiho (Kamehameha IV) were there. The Hawaiian words used as a Christmas greeting changed sixteen times from 1876 to 1903. "Merry Christmas" was first stated with the words *Ka Nupepe Ku'oko'a*. The greeting today is *Mele Kalikimaka*.

Boats were the first link, over thousands of ocean miles, from Hawaii to the mainland. However, settlement in the western states needed more than boats, which depended upon water. It needed railroads. Chinese migration to California increased dramatically. Chinese laborers were brought to California to help build them. When railroads finally linked the East and West Coasts, horsepower was replaced by train power.

Toys usually reflect our history. The railroad's importance was most obvious in the early 1900s when the Lionel Train Company created unique detailed model trains. These trains soon became one of the most popular Christmas gifts.

An early cultural influence in California came from Spanish explorers. *Cascarones*, or brightly colored eggshells filled with confetti, perfume, gold dust, or favors, were a California Christmas Eve tradition reflecting this culture. *Cascarones* were crushed above the head of the girl you wished to compliment, showering her with the contents.

Rosemary and lavender leaves were scattered on floors of *adobes*, as Spanish homes in Monterey were called. The fragrance from people walking on the leaves was a reminder of a legend. The tale tells us that there was no scent from these herbs until Mary washed her holy infant's clothes and hung them to dry on bushes nearby. Today the aroma of hot Mexican chocolate, spiced with cinnamon and vanilla, mingles with the scent of herbs at Christmastime.

Christmas at the White House

Holiday seasons in the early years of the White House were quiet and in keeping with mixed religious feelings about celebrating Christmas. Thomas Jefferson barely mentioned the holiday in his December letters. However, on Christmas Day President Jefferson left his office in the White House to choose the goose for Christmas dinner.

A White House Winter

President Andrew Jackson took office in 1829, as Americans began to move toward purchasing gifts rather than making them, and using store-bought decorations in both home and public buildings. President Jackson's children invited guests to a "frolic in the East Room, and a visit from Santa." The White House chef created a delightful decoration. A table in the shape of a Maltese cross was topped with a pyramid of cotton snowballs. Combined in the chef's creation were colored icicles, fruits and vegetables, cakes, candles, all types of cookies, candies, and toy animals. The pyramid was topped with a game-cock, its wings outspread. After dinner children played with the cotton snowballs in the East Room.

Gifts come to the White House in many forms. The Lincolns were given a live turkey for one Christmas dinner. The Lincolns' son Tad named the turkey Jack and taught him to follow behind him. His father reminded Tad that the turkey was sent to them for their Christmas dinner. The turkey was finally spared when Lincoln gave Jack a formal Christmas presidential pardon. President Lincoln purchased toy soldiers for Tad from a small Washington toy store. Lincoln once said, "I want to give him all the toys I did not have. . . ."

Charles Dickens

Washington Irving

White House entertainment today may be provided by movie stars or well-known musicians. In the holiday season of 1842 two famous authors, Charles Dickens and Washington Irving, were invited to the White House of President John Tyler. Dickens's *A Christmas Carol,* published in 1842, was written after his visit to the United States.

Not all U.S. presidents have been wealthy. As a new president, Ulysses Grant had to pawn his pocket watch to buy Christmas presents for his family. Even though he was struggling financially, he was an excellent host during the holiday season of 1874. The first foreign head of state, the king of Hawaii, was a guest at the White House. Elaborate dinners had as many as twenty-nine courses.

Some books mention the first Christmas tree in the White House during the term of Franklin Pierce in 1856. However, most people feel the first White House Christmas tree was during the 1889–1893 term of President Benjamin Harrison. A grandchild, "Baby" Benjamin Harrison McKee, lived in the White House with his mother and baby sister, Mary. Baby Benjamin was frequently the center of attention. Reports of the Harrisons' Christmas celebration in 1889 included a description of greenery, gifts, candy, and nuts placed throughout the upper apartments. The president dressed as Santa and distributed gifts from under the candle-lighted tree.

only 4,999 to go!

The first official observance of Christmas as a holiday was in 1885, when Congress established Christmas Day as a paid holiday for federal workers. That same year organizations and schools were contacted to assist with the five thousand ornaments needed to decorate the first official White House tree. President Grover Cleveland, the only president to have a child born in the White House, helped reduce some of the fire danger in 1895 when he allowed electric lights to replace candles on the tree. One of the Cleveland girls found a small dollhouse, which looked like the White House, under the Christmas tree. Following the establishment of a Christmas tree tradition, we have had an official tree every year since 1889.

The teddy bear, still found under many Christmas trees today, was designed to honor President Theodore Roosevelt's act of saving a bear's life during a hunting trip. Stuffed bears were first designed as decorations in a stationery and novelty store. The store owner received permission from Mr. Roosevelt to name the bears "teddy bears." President Roosevelt was opposed to cutting trees and had to be reassured that harvesting pine trees for Christmas was environmentally sound.

An enormous mince pie was served during the Christmas season when William Howard Taft was president. A family in New Jersey presented the president with a mince pie that measured three feet across and six feet in circumference. It was two and one half inches deep.

President Calvin Coolidge started the custom of lighting a tree outside the White House in 1923. Called the Nation's Tree, each year it can be seen on the Ellipse, just beyond the South Lawn. There are also fifty-seven smaller trees representing each state; the territories of American Samoa, Guam, Puerto Rico, and the Virgin Islands; and the District of Columbia. The holiday season officially opens when the forty-thousand lights of our Nation's Tree are first turned on.

Music is also an integral part of the Christmas celebration at the White House. On December 24, 1929, President Herbert Hoover was hosting a dinner party when a siren sounded. The band continued to play as an aide rushed in to tell of a fire in the executive offices. The president and his guests watched from outside, in the snow, while the fire department put out the fire.

Each presidential family sets the tone for entertaining in the White House. Pat Nixon planned more formal social events. She started candlelight evening tours of the White House. Betty Ford expanded this idea by initiating one evening for senior citizens, another evening for families of White House staff, and two evenings for the public. Musical activities during the holiday season may include the U.S. Army Chorus singing or a performance by the U.S. Marine Band.

President and Mrs. Jimmy Carter celebrated their first White House Christmas in 1977. All ornaments were handmade, many created by mentally disabled adults and children. Decorations included strings of peanuts from President Carter's home state of Georgia and corn-husk dolls from Iowa. A Victorian theme for decorations was developed for the 1980 Christmas.

The creation of a gingerbread house follows a tradition started in 1969. The White House chef in 1981 honored President Ronald Reagan's love for jelly beans by including a jelly bean chimney, and he added illuminated windows. The three-foot-tall house included figures of Hansel, Gretel, a witch, and a snowman. The Reagans had a Christmas card list of seventy-five thousand names.

The bicentennial Christmas of 1976 included a White House tree decorated with more than twenty-five hundred handmade flowers, including the state flowers of all fifty states. The bicentennial theme for tree decorations was Tchaikovsky's ballet *The Nutcracker*. These unique decorations included fifty pairs of ballet slippers, porcelain dancers, a silk flower representing each state, and historic glass ornaments from the White House collection.

The 1991 Christmas tree of President George H. W. Bush and Mrs. Bush featured needlepoint tree ornaments, red glass balls, a turn-of-the-century needlepoint village, and figures from Noah's ark. In 1994 a seventy-pound gingerbread house was designed by White House chefs to look like President Bill Clinton's boyhood home in Arkansas.

President George W. Bush and Mrs. Bush decorated the White House tree with ornaments by artists from all fifty states and the District of Columbia. These ornaments were miniature replicas of historic houses from the artists' regions.

In the future, who knows what new traditions presidents and their families will bring to the White House and the nation. It is certain that these festivities will be as colorful and memorable as those of presidents past.

Christmas at the Post Office

Our Christmas stamps add a second message to each envelope by opening the door to our history and culture. Think of the joy early western settlers would have felt if they could have received Christmas cards and letters from friends and relatives left in the East. Although postal service had been established for eastern states, very little overland mail found its way west until April 1860, when Pony Express mail service began operation between Saint Louis, Missouri, and Sacramento, California. The Central Overland California and Pike's Peak Express Company operated this service for only one year. When the transcontinental telegraph was completed in 1861, messages could be sent in minutes, and so the Pony Express was no longer needed.

In the 1850s an American, Richard H. Pease, printed a simple white card illustrated with yuletide birds and animals. Louis Prang, a Prussian immigrant, later improved on that first American Christmas card. The cards were expensive, but they were unique. Some were cut in a star or diamond shape. One card depicted "snow" made from tiny pieces of blown glass.

Christmas cards can't be mailed without stamps. It normally takes several months to print and distribute the more than two billion stamps now needed to meet customer demands during the holiday mailing season. First issued in 1962, Christmas stamps were an experiment designed to speed mail delivery during the postal service's busiest time of year. Perhaps the post office hoped people would purchase stamps and mail Christmas cards in early December. The experiment must have been successful, because Christmas stamps are now issued each year.

Some people want a unique Christmas-related postmark on their Christmas cards. They send their cards to be postmarked and mailed from post offices in cities such as North Pole, Alaska; Snowflake, Arizona; Bethlehem in the states of Connecticut, Georgia, Indiana, Maryland, and Pennsylvania; Santa, Idaho; Santa Claus, Indiana; Christmas, Michigan; Silver Star, Montana; Christmas Valley, Oregon; and Bells, Texas.

Christmas stamps have a rich heritage and provide opportunities to look at traditional images of Christmas in the United States. Subjects have included holly, mistletoe, and other Christmas flowers. Both religious and traditional subjects have been used. What was the picture on the stamp issued the year you were born?

A committee determines eligibility of subjects for commemoration on U.S. stamps. Christmas is one of the themes that may have a stamp designed to recognize this tradition. If you have a subject that meets the criteria, you can write to:

Citizens' Stamp Advisory Committee
c/o Stamp Management
U.S. Postal Service
475 L'Enfant Plaza, SW, Room 4474EB
Washington, DC 20260-6756

Fun Things to Do

I have learned that the gift of time is more important than anything you can purchase. By giving a gift of time, or of kind words, you give a gift of self. These are unique, and will be remembered, both in the heart *and* in the head of the recipient. Family and friends remember Christmas celebrations, not for the money spent or the gifts purchased.

Create a bibliography of Christmas books. Make a copy of the bibliography and give the list as a gift. Plan to give your own "reading," just as Charles Dickens did. Your reading can be for a younger child or an older friend.

Find the telephone number for a museum in your area and report their holiday activities to your classroom and family.

Interview older relatives about their childhood Christmas memories. Write and illustrate stories told to you. Make a book about family Christmases of the past. This unique gift will please everyone in your family. Use a long, narrow piece of paper and create a time line of events, birth dates, addresses, and celebrations. Begin the time line with the oldest person in your family.

Ask friends who speak another language to teach you a Christmas song in their language.

Work with friends to learn Christmas carols. Have one person act, or pantomime, the song while others sing the words.

Memorize Christmas poems and recite them to older or younger friends.

Crafts

Christmas Journal

Choose a spiral-bound or three-ring loose-leaf notebook. Include the date and location of the Christmas you describe. Who was there? Who didn't come? Did they call or fax or e-mail? You can go back in time by asking grandparents, aunts, and uncles about their childhood Christmases. Use all your senses when you write. Describe the look in the eyes of younger relatives when they first see the lights of the Christmas tree. Record recipes and the taste of your favorite cookie. Illustrate your Christmas journal with drawings or with pictures clipped from magazines. Describe your part in a school Christmas program or a special church event. Include Christmas cards, a picture from a catalog of a gift you hope to receive, and the best thing that occurred during the holiday. The gift of remembering, through writing, is a gift you give yourself, to be enjoyed for many tomorrows.

A Festive Pomander

Pomander is from the French words *pomme d'ambre*, apple of amber or ambergris. Many years ago people carried a sweet-smelling ball made of perfumed ingredients, including ambergris, which was used to create perfume. The pomander was worn or carried in a perforated case in order to ward off infection or counteract bad smells. The cases, usually made of gold or silver, were also called pomanders. Today we make pomanders as Christmas decorations and as gifts to hang in closets or cabinets with linens. It's important to make your pomander early, as it will take one month to dry.

You will need:

1 thin-skinned fresh orange, about 11″ in circumference	2 pins with large colored heads
1-ounce box of whole cloves	2 strips of paper, 1/4″ wide x 11″ long
2-ounce package of orrisroot powder (can be found in drugstores and health-food stores)	3 pieces of tissue paper (12″ x 12″)
	small paper bag
	mixing bowl
2 ounces of cinnamon powder	teaspoon
2 yards of 1/4″-wide ribbons in 2 different colors	small 8-penny nail

Wear an apron or old shirt. Place newspapers over your work area.

1: Cross the two strips of paper and pin through them onto the top of the orange. Pin their ends to the bottom of the orange. The orange is now divided into four sections.

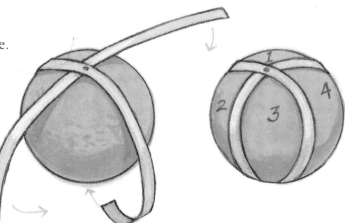

2: Use the nail to make holes in the skin of the orange.

3: Put cloves into the holes. Push each clove's point in all the way up to the head of the clove.

4: Put the cloves close together.

5: In a mixing bowl mix orrisroot and cinnamon.

6: Roll the orange in the mixture until it is totally coated. The powder should be firmly pressed down between the lines of cloves.

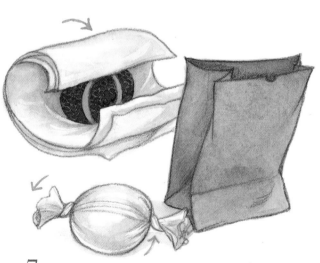

7: Carefully place the orange on three layers of tissue paper, add any powder left in the bowl, and roll up the orange, twisting the paper at each end. Put the wrapped orange into a small paper bag.

8: Put the bag into a dry, dark place such as a closet. The orange must dry out for at least one month. If it is not allowed to dry completely, it will rot.

9: After a month, remove the paper strips. Cross the two lengths of ribbon and sit the pomander in the middle. Tie the ends of one ribbon on the top of the orange. Do the same with the other ribbon.

10: Make a bow with one set of ends and knot the other two ends to make a loop.

Christmas Stamp Picture

Purchase a block of four Christmas stamps. Make a frame for the stamps by covering a piece of cardboard with a small piece of solid-colored wrapping paper. Use a narrow piece of colored tape to cover the edge of the cardboard and wrapping paper. Adhere the stamps to the cardboard. Glue a small piece of string on the back. This can be used as a gift or as a tree decoration.

Peanut Plant

Several weeks before Christmas, place a raw peanut on a shallow clay saucer (normally used under a clay pot) or in a small glass jar. The bottom of the jar or saucer should be covered with a layer of wet cotton balls. Place the peanut on the cotton. The peanut will sprout and make a leafy gift. Tie a ribbon on the container to add color.

wet cotton ball

keep moist

Cascarones

According to legend, *cascaron*, a Spanish word meaning shell or peel, can be traced to the Renaissance. In those times the empty eggshells were filled with perfumed powder and given to women as gifts. The wife of Emperor Maximillian of Spain brought the tradition to Mexico in the mid-1800s. The perfumed powder was replaced with confetti. For some people the *cascaron* holds religious significance. The eggshell represents the empty tomb of Christ. The confetti represents the joy and celebration of Christ's resurrection. *Cascarones* are popular both at Christmas and Easter.

How to make *cascarones*:

1: Carefully make a dime-sized opening at one end of an egg.

3: Wash the eggshell and allow to dry.

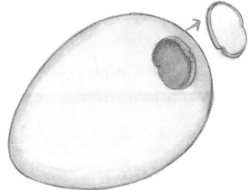

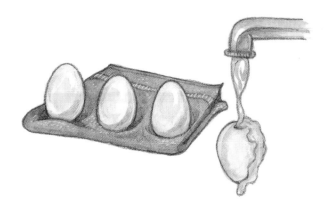

2: Drain the egg contents from the shell through the opening. (The contents can be used to make scrambled eggs.)

4: Dip the empty eggshell into diluted food coloring or commercial egg dye.

5: After the shell is dry, use crayons, paints, and markers to decorate it. You can also use glue and sprinkle glitter over the glue.

7: Glue a small piece of tissue paper over the hole.

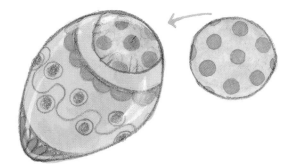

6: Use a small spoon or funnel to pour confetti into the eggshell. The *cascaron* can also be filled with birdseed.

Smashing the *cascaron* should be a surprise. It can be done on an unsuspecting person's head or placed inside someone's collar so that the confetti trickles into his or her clothes.

Santa's Hat Button Game

For each hat you will need:

1 8" dinner plate
sheets of red and white construction paper
10" piece of string, knotted at one end
1 cotton ball
1 button (about 1" across)
glue, scissors, tape

1: Cut a half-circle shape from the red paper, using the plate as a guide. Connect the paper, and tape to make a cone.

2: Glue a band of white paper around the large end of the cone.

3: Cut a small bit from the end of the cone and thread the string through.

4: Tie the button to the end of the string outside the hat. And glue the cotton ball to the end of the cone.

5: The button is dangling from the string.

See if you can swing the button up and catch it in the hat.

Homemade Christmas Cards

Materials:

any heavy paper such as index stock, tag board, construction paper, Bristol board, or lightweight cardboard

paper, lace, bits of ribbon; dried flowers, leaves, or ferns; border designs; glitter; foil; metallic paper; soft fabric; wallpaper; stickers; gummed stars; doilies for decoration

To fold the cards, consider:

1: A regular book fold

2: A top-down fold

3: A top-down fold with the top shorter

4: A three-panel fold with sides folded in

5: A regular fold with a window cut in the front

Before folding, you will want to plan the card to fit an available envelope or one you make. To deckle the paper edges for cards, use a heavy paper (construction or watercolor).

1: Draw a line along the edge to be deckled.

2: Paint a water strip between that line and the edge of the card. Turn the card over and do the same thing on the back of the first water line. When the paper is saturated, place a ruler along the line and tear the paper upward. Smooth down the edge and allow to dry.

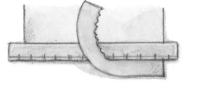

Smooth edge

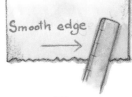

Cranberry Garland

For a cranberry garland you will need:
5 kumquats
50 whole cloves
70 cranberries for each yard of wire
medium gauge floral wire

1: Push cloves one by one into the kumquats to form a ring around the middle of each fruit.

2: Thread the cranberries onto a reel of wire, adding a studded kumquat after nine or ten cranberries.

3: Continue threading cranberries and kumquats until the garland is the desired length.

4: To finish, bend large loops in the ends of the wire to prevent the fruit from sliding off the ends.

Popcorn Strings

Plain, day-old popcorn can be strung on dental floss with a needle. Each length of floss should be about three feet. Working with short lengths of floss will keep it from becoming tangled. These lengths can be tied together to form a long string for the tree.

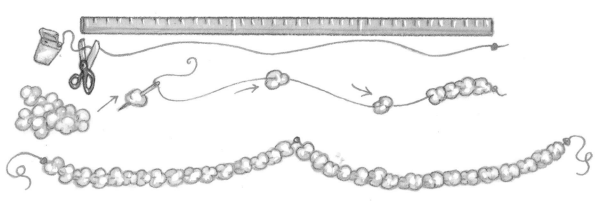

Christmas Tree Decorations

Buy prepared cookie dough at the supermarket or make your own dough. Preheat the oven to 350°.

1: Lightly flour a flat surface and roll dough to a thickness of one-quarter inch.

2: Dip cookie cutter in flour and cut out shapes. Before baking, sprinkle the cookies with granulated sugar to make them glitter.

·3: Place cookies on baking sheet at least one inch apart. Bake for about six minutes, until golden brown.

4: Remove from oven and, while cookies are still on the cookie sheet, use a soda straw to make a hole for yarn or ribbon. (Do not place the hole too close to the edge of the cookie.) Cool cookies on sheet for about three minutes. Move to a rack to continue to cool.

straw

5: Once cookies have cooled, place colored yarn or Christmas ribbon through the hole to form a loop for hanging on the tree.

tie

Recipes

Christmas *Bischochitos,* or Aniseed Cookies

Sometimes spelled *Bizchochitos*—"small biscuits"—these cookies are a Christmas tradition in New Mexico. They may be shaped into a round cookie or cut out.

1 cup butter or margarine

2¼ cups all-purpose flour

3 drops anise flavoring

1 egg

1 cup sugar

1 tablespoon milk

1 teaspoon baking powder

1 teaspoon vanilla

pinch of salt

1 teaspoon cinnamon

2 tablespoons sugar

Preheat oven to 375°.

Combine 1 teaspoon ground cinnamon and 2 tablespoons sugar and set aside.

Cream butter or margarine. Add *half* the flour and the anise, egg, sugar, milk, baking powder, vanilla, and salt. Beat until combined. Beat in remaining flour. Divide dough in half. Cover and refrigerate for 3 hours. On lightly floured surface, roll each half of dough to ⅛-inch thickness. Cut with your favorite cutter. Place on ungreased cookie sheet. Sprinkle sugar-cinnamon mix on cookies. Bake in 375° oven 6 to 8 minutes until bottoms are lightly browned. Cool. Makes 36 to 48 cookies.

Double Peanut Cookies

1 cup butter or margarine

1 cup peanut butter

1 cup sugar

1 cup brown sugar

2 eggs

1 teaspoon vanilla

2¼ cups all-purpose flour

2 teaspoons baking soda

½ teaspoon salt

1½ cups salted peanuts

Preheat oven to 350°.

Chop peanuts. In a mixing bowl cream together butter, peanut butter, sugar, and brown sugar; beat in eggs and vanilla. In a separate bowl, stir together flour, baking soda, and salt; blend into creamed mixture. Stir in chopped peanuts. Form dough into 1-inch balls. Place on ungreased cookie sheet; flatten slightly with fingers. Bake at 350° about 10 minutes. Makes 72 cookies.

Nut Crescents

Rich pastries of central European and Norse families were favorites of those who settled the Great Lakes area. One of these is a cookie called Nut Crescents, which is similar to American cookies called sandies, Mexican wedding cakes, and Russian tea cakes.

1 cup butter or margarine

½ cup sugar

1 teaspoon vanilla

2 cups all-purpose flour

½ cup ground walnuts

sifted powdered sugar

Preheat oven to 325°.

Cream together butter or margarine, sugar, and vanilla. Stir in a small amount of flour at a time. Mix in the walnuts. Using about 2 teaspoons dough for each, shape into crescents. Place on ungreased baking sheet. Bake at 325° for 20 minutes. Remove from baking sheet. While cookies are slightly warm, sift powdered sugar over them. Makes 4 dozen.

Colonists' Scripture Cake

Many activities in the colonies were related to the Bible. This old recipe, based on books of the Bible, makes baking like a treasure hunt.

Cream ½ cup Judges 5:25 till light
Blend in ¾ cup Jeremiah 6:20
Stir together 2 cups I Kings 4:22
½ teaspoon Amos 4:5
And II Chronicles 9:9
Dash Leviticus 2:13

Mix 3 Jeremiah 17:11
½ cup Judges 4:19
⅓ cup I Samuel 14:25
Stir in 1 cup I Samuel 30:12
1 cup Nahum 3:12
½ cup Numbers 17:8

Bake at 325° for 40 minutes. Brush all sides with Proverbs 31:6.

42

Today's Scripture Cake

$1/2$ cup butter or margarine

$3/4$ cup molasses

2 cups all-purpose flour

$1/2$ teaspoon baking soda

$1/2$ teaspoon ground cinnamon

$1/4$ teaspoon ground cloves

a pinch of ground ginger

dash of salt

3 eggs well beaten

$1/2$ cup buttermilk

$1/3$ cup honey

1 cup raisins

1 cup chopped dried figs

$1/2$ cup chopped almonds

$1/2$ cup orange juice

Preheat oven to 325°.

In large mixing bowl, cream butter and blend in molasses. Stir flour, baking soda, cinnamon, cloves, ginger, and salt together. Combine eggs, buttermilk, and honey. Add egg mixture and dry ingredients alternately to creamed mixture. Mix well. Stir in raisins, figs, and almonds. Turn mixture into greased and floured 9-x-5-x-3-inch loaf pan. Bake at 325° for 40 minutes. Cover loosely with foil. Bake 50 minutes more. Let cool in pan for about 10 minutes; remove from pan. Cool on rack; brush all sides with orange juice. Wrap in foil and store 1 to 2 days in refrigerator. Makes 1 loaf.

Time Line of Toys

In the 1800s there were *no* video games! In fact, there was no television. The first soft, furry teddy bear was still unknown. Children were happy to receive an orange, a sweet, or a handmade toy.

This Christmas create a toy time line for your entire family. Look at the following time line of toys. Ask brothers, sisters, parents, and grandparents to describe toys they received at Christmas. Did they receive a toy or a game? Did they play Chinese checkers or dominoes? What games did they play? Did they ever receive a top, marbles, jacks, paper dolls, or pick-up sticks?

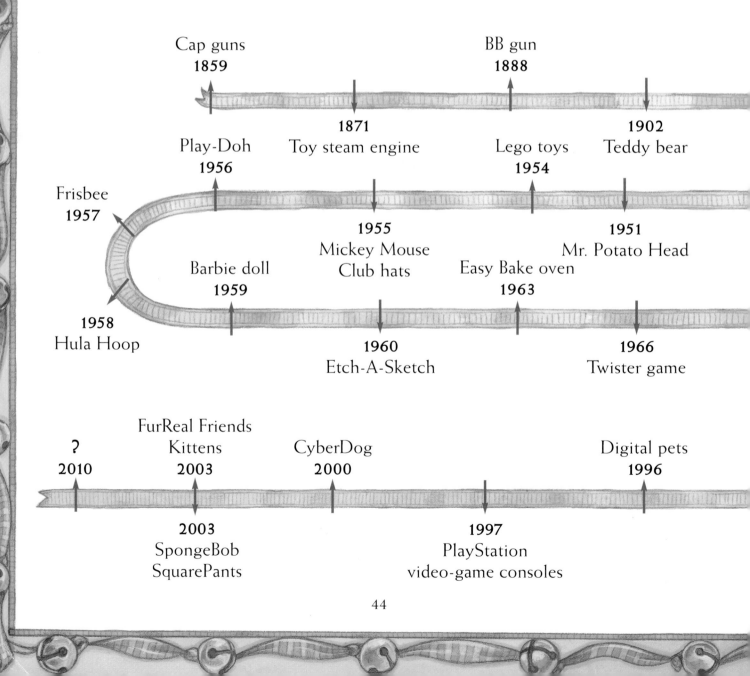

Cap guns
1859

BB gun
1888

1871
Toy steam engine

Lego toys
1954

1902
Teddy bear

Play-Doh
1956

Frisbee
1957

1955
Mickey Mouse
Club hats

1951
Mr. Potato Head

Barbie doll
1959

Easy Bake oven
1963

1958
Hula Hoop

1960
Etch-A-Sketch

1966
Twister game

FurReal Friends
Kittens
2003

?
2010

CyberDog
2000

Digital pets
1996

2003
SpongeBob
SquarePants

1997
PlayStation
video-game consoles

44

Books may have been given as gifts. Books are not toys; however, in years past, and today, the gift of a book remains a treasure. Books for children in the 1897 Sears Roebuck catalog included *Aesop's Fables*, *Black Beauty*, *Gulliver's Travels*, and titles written by Louisa May Alcott. What books have you or family members received in Christmases past?

Determine the approximate year someone received a certain book or toy. Add your own gifts to the time line. This will be a wonderful record for you to reread in Christmases in the future. Dates shown in this time line indicate the first year these toys were for sale.

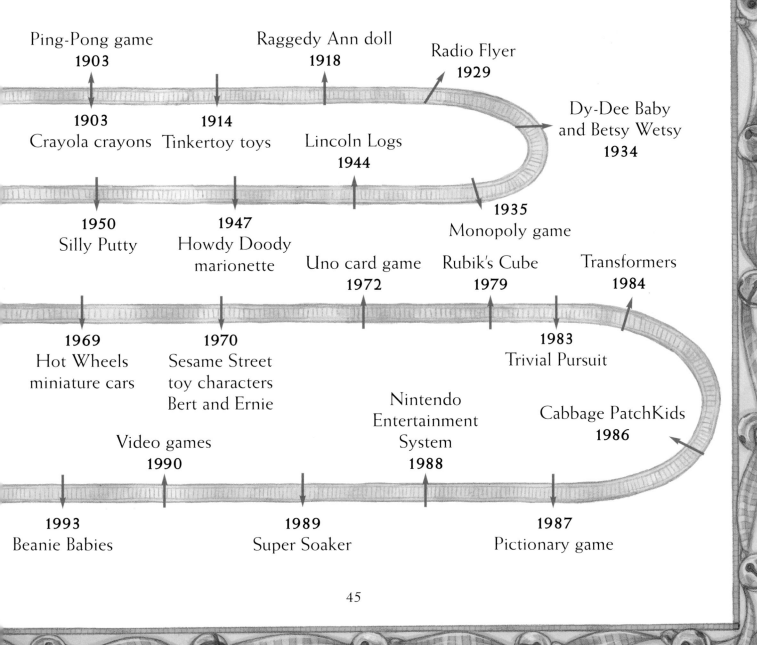

 # Bibliography

Askawa, Gil. *The Toy Book*. New York: Knopf, 1992.

Better Homes and Gardens Heritage Cook Book. Des Moines, IA: Meredith Corporation, 1975.

Blumberg, Rhoda. *Full Steam Ahead: The Race to Build a Transcontinental Railroad*. Washington, DC: National Geographic Society, 1996.

"Bonfires in Louisiana Light the Way for Santa Claus's Sleigh." *The Dallas Morning News*, December 8, 2002.

Brewer's Dictionary of Phrase & Fable. New York: Harper & Row, 1970.

Cohen, Hennig, and Tristram Potter Coffin. *America Celebrates! A Patchwork of Weird & Wonderful Holiday Lore*. Detroit, MI: Visible Ink, 1991.

Cross, Gary. *Kids' Stuff: Toys and the Changing World of American Childhood*. Cambridge, MA: Harvard University Press, 1997.

Fisher, Leonard Everett. *Tracks Across America: The Story of the American Railroad, 1825–1900*. New York: Holiday House, 1992.

Ford, Marianne. *Copycats & Artifacts: 42 Creative Artisan Projects to Make*. Boston: Godine, 1986.

Gale Encyclopedia of Multicultural America. Detroit, MI: Gale Research, 1995.

The Great Idea Finder. www.ideafinder.com

Gulevich, Ranya. *Encyclopedia of Christmas*. Detroit, MI: Omnigraphics, 2000.

Henderson, Yorke. *Christmas Holiday Book*. New York: Parents' Magazine Press, 1952.

Johnson, Sylvia A. *Tomatoes, Potatoes, Corn, and Beans: How the Foods of the Americas Changed Eating Around the World*. New York: Atheneum, 1997.

Kroll, Stephen. *Pony Express!* New York: Scholastic, 1996.

McComas, Tom, and James Tuohy. *Lionel: A Collector's Guide and History, Postwar*, vol. 2. Wilmette, IL: TM Productions, 1978.

Marrin, Albert. *Struggle for a Continent: The French and Indian Wars, 1690–1760*. New York: Atheneum, 1987.

Metcalfe, Edna. *The Trees of Christmas*. Nashville, TN: Abingdon, 1969.

Nathan, Joan. *An American Folklife Cookbook*. New York: Schocken, 1984.

National Geographic Picture Atlas of Our World. Washington, DC: National Geographic Society, 1990.

National Toy Hall of Fame, Strong Museum, Rochester, NY. www.strongmuseum.org

Nissenbaum, Stephen. *The Battle for Christmas*. New York: Knopf, 1996.

Pierce, Neal R. *The Great Plains States of America: People, Politics, and Power in the Nine Great Plains States*. New York: W. W. Norton, 1973.

The Pillsbury Family Christmas Cookbook. Minneapolis, MN: The Pillsbury Company, 1966.

Relph, Ingeborg, and Penny Stanway. *Christmas: A Cook's Tour*. Oxford, England: A Lion Book, 1991.

Restad, Penne L. *Christmas in America: A History*. New York: Oxford University Press, 1995.

Richter's Anchor Blocks. www.chem.sunysb.edu/msl/LEGO/anchor.html

Ross, Nancy Wilson. *Westward the Women*. San Francisco: North Point, 1985.

Rozin, Elisabeth. *Blue Corn and Chocolate*. New York: Knopf, 1992.

Schlesinger, Arthur M., Jr., and Mark C. Carnes, eds. *A History of American Life*, rev. and abridged. New York: Scribner, 1996.

Schlissel, Lillian, Byrd Gibbens, and Elizabeth Hampsten. *Far from Home: Families of the Westward Journey*. New York: Schocken, 1989.

Schmidt, Leigh Eric. *Consumer Rites: The Buying & Selling of American Holidays*. Princeton, NJ: Princeton University Press, 1995.

Shumway, George, and Howard C. Frey. *Conestoga Wagon, 1750–1850: Freight Carrier for 100 Years of America's Westward Expansion*, 3rd ed. York, PA: G. Shumway, 1968.

Snyder, Phillip V. *The Christmas Tree Book: The History of the Christmas Tree and Antique Christmas Tree Ornaments*. New York: Viking, 1976.

Straach, Kathryn. "In These Cities, the Holiday Mood Is Light." *The Dallas Morning News*, November 17, 2002.

Strawbery Banke, Portsmouth, New Hampshire. www.strawberybanke.org

Thompson, Sue Ellen. *Holiday Symbols*, 2nd ed. Detroit, MI: Omnigraphics, 2000.

Werner, Emmy E. *Pioneer Children on the Journey West*. Boulder, CO: Westview, 1995.

Wexler, Sanford, ed. *Westward Expansion: An Eyewitness History*. New York: Facts on File, 1991.

Index